The guide to becoming rich slowly and never having to work again

The Most Effective Ways to Make Money Passively

Copyright © 2016 R.O. Sawyer III. All rights reserved.

Cover credit: SelfPubBookCovers.com/Saphira

No part of this book may be reproduced or transmitted in any form or by any means, electronic or mechanical, including photocopying, recording, or by any information storage and retrieval system, without permission in writing from the author.

TABLE OF CONTENTS

CHAPTERS **PAGE**

Introduction
Chapter 1 – Invest in Stocks for Dividends
Chapter 2 – Buy a Rental Property
Chapter 3 – Earn Royalties
Chapter 4 – Earn Interest
Chapter 5 – Sell Yourself
Chapter 6 – Start A Blog
Chapter 7 – Drop Ship
Chapter 8 – Earn Commissions Through Affiliate Marketing
Chapter 9 – Sell Products On Niche Sites
Chapter 10 – Selling Information Products
Conclusion

Introduction

One definition of passive income is "business that generates income after you have invested your time, money and energy." I agree, with one caveat: you do need to do some maintenance from time to time in order to keep things running smoothly.

I don't believe in overnight achievement. There's always a great deal of diligent work and time put in beforehand. For example, Angry Birds may seem like an overnight success, but it was the 52nd game that Rovio made, and it took about 18 months post-release to gain a sizable audience.

There is no such thing as 100% automated income. With real estate you need to manage your properties, and with the stock market you need to manage your portfolio. An online business can take even more time.

I am sure that there is no viable get-rich-quick scheme anywhere on earth. Successful people always pay the price in time and effort. You truly can make money in your sleep, but only after you've exhausted yourself working for it.

Many people think that passive income is money that comes to you with zero effort. What a lazy mindset. We're always taught that hard work pays off, right? So why should passive income be an exception?

That's the one thing that most people don't know about passive income: how much effort it requires beforehand. The good news is that it's perfectly true that, once you have a passive income system set up, it requires relatively little effort to continue generating those dollars.

In this book I'm going to talk about ten things you can do, with some effort on your part, to get yourself to that place.

Happy reading!

Chapter 1 – Invest in Stocks for Dividends

After you purchase stock you can profit by both the increase in value of the company and the dividend income stream. I'm going to concentrate on dividends here, as they're more firmly identified with passive income.

A dividend is essentially your share of the company's profits. You don't have a part in managing the company; you're only a part owner. The company pays others to manage its business, which generates the profits; you simply collect the dividend checks.

When you're choosing stock with an eye to dividends, a good approach is to take a look at historical dividend yield. Dividend yield is the ratio of the dividend paid for each share over the price per share.

A higher number is better, as it shows that a company pays a higher dividend for each dollar invested it. According to the AFR Share Tables, the normal dividend yield on 200 of the biggest Australian companies was around 5.5%. This implies that for each $1,000 invested you would receive $55.

Types of Dividends

Dividends are distributions of a company's profits to its shareholders. They can be money, stock or property. Most investors prefer money dividends, of course. But stock dividends can be very profitable over the long haul; if the company's value increases, you can make a large profit selling the shares.

Below are the types of dividends

Cash Dividends

Cash dividends are fairly simple. Shareholders of record receive them by check or electronic transfer according to how many shares they own. To pay money dividends, a company must satisfy two conditions: It must have positive income, and it must have enough cash on hand.

For instance, say you own 2,000 shares of regular stock in XYZ Corporation. XYZ has both a pile of cash and a positive income, so the board of directors chooses to pay a cash dividend of $10 per share. Your profit is $20,000 (2,000 shares × $10).

Property Dividends

In this case, the company issues a dividend comprising one of its assets. This could be anything: equipment, vehicles, inventory, whatever.

When a company issues a property dividend, it needs to state the value of the asset as its reasonable worth.

Stock Dividends

Companies typically issue stock dividends when they're low on working capital but need to toss their investors a bone. Although no cash changes hands, stock dividends are distributed the same way as money dividends: Each shareholder of record gets a number of additional shares based on how many shares that shareholder already owns.

This dividend is communicated as a percentage instead of a dollar sum. For instance, a company might issue a stock dividend of 5 percent, and an investor who owned 1,500 shares would get an extra 75 shares of stock (1,500 × .05).

Another kind of stock share that doesn't decrease profit is a stock split. A stock split increases the number of shares outstanding by issuing more shares to present stockholders according to the number they currently own. Stock splits are normally done when a company feels the cost of its stock is too high, because they have the effect of lowering the price per share.

For example, suppose XYZ Corporation stock is trading for $100, and the company feels this high value decreases investors' appetite for the stock. To get the cost of the stock down to $25 per share, the company performs a four-for-one split. Each outstanding share is now equivalent to four shares.

How to earn passive income from stock investing through dividends

Investing for dividend income is a time-honored system that is demonstrably remunerative. Of course, the investor must keep good tabs on his or her investments to avoid potentially enormous losses. Dividend investing can work exceptionally well as a retirement strategy since it provides a fairly steady income when done correctly.

Selecting Stocks that Pay Dividends

Research stocks that are known for paying steady dividends

You can find this information in the Saturday edition of the Wall Street Journal, where the stock quotes display a YLD. The number found in this section is the annualized rate. (Other sources include Morningstar's DividendInvestor, the online bulletin Dividend Detective, and weekly updates in the Value Line Investment Survey that can be found at your local library.)

The dividend yield is different from the dividend rate. The dividend yield is the ratio of the dividend paid for each share over the price per share. The dividend rate is the total amount of cash you can hope to get from a share in one year.

Put resources into stocks that give high dividends consistently

Buy stock in companies that have had high profits over the last five years and have a history of paying high dividends. Companies that are still developing will reinvest much of their income, but established companies (for example, Procter & Gamble, Coca-Cola and 3M) usually issue dividends instead.

Let's examine AT&T. A one time a share of AT&T sold at $25 and paid a dividend of 40 cents like clockwork. Any investor purchasing 1,000 shares would have spent $25,000 and received $400 ever quarter, besides any appreciation in the value of the stock. Over ten years, the stockholder could expect to receive $16,000.

The board of directors can raise or lower a company's dividends, which is why you need to pick a stable company with a strong history of paying rising (or at least steady) dividends.

Research different factors

Besides the dividends, there are a couple of other things to look at when seeking a solid company worth your investment.

Invest in a company that has a lower obligation load (liabilities) than its associates or its industry average. This gives it the flexibility to borrow if necessary to bolster operations and dividends. This data can be found in the company's annual report, which is usually available on its website.

Look up the company's profit per share. This can also be found in the annual report. Contrast it with the income per share. The company's profit per share ought to be close to 80% of its income per share. In the event that a company makes $0.25/share and is paying a dividend of $0.50/share, for instance, this is not an indication of good financial condition.

Check the company's current ratio. This is the proportion of current resources to current liabilities, and it quantifies a company's capacity to meet present commitments. Again, it will be in the annual report. Put your money into a company that has a considerable amount of its own. If a company's current ratio is more than 1, it's in great financial shape.

Purchase the stock

You can do this by setting up an online trading account, for example, with Motif Investing, TradeKing, Scottrade, or OptionsHouse. Make sure you understand the fees you will be charged before you choose a site. Alternatively, you could work with a stockbroker at a firm like TD Ameritrade or Fidelity.

Track and calculate dividend yield

This is the ratio of the annual dividend per share over the present price per share. For instance, if stock XYZ has a share price of $50 and an annualized dividend of $1.00, its yield is .02 or 2%. This data can be found on the company's website. Don't just look at the number, though; a high dividend yield may reflect a presently low stock cost resulting from temporary issues. Give careful consideration to the long-term profit trend.

A company with a history of paying a reliably growing or steady dividend is ideal. Be very careful about an outfit that has needed to decrease its dividend. Sometimes there is a good explanation for this, but if you can't find one, look elsewhere for your investment.

Calculate dividend coverage ratio

Take the company's one-year net profit and subtract the dividends paid on irredeemable preferred shares. Divide this by the most recent one-year dividend on ordinary shares. (All of this data can be found on the company's annual report on their website.) A company with a ratio of 1.0 or better is viewed as "protected," and a 3.0, for instance, implies that a company has enough income to pay dividends up to three times the present dividend payout.

When you do invest in stock, spend considerably less than you make and pay yourself first. Dedicate part of your other income to investing, but leave yourself plenty to live on. Aim to have your investment to return significantly more than your fixed expenses every year so you can reinvest the excess in more stock.

Keep up to a year of living expenses in cash and currency market funds. This isn't only for a backup in case of emergency; it will also smooth out the good and bad times for your investments. If they don't yield as expected for a quarter or two, your emergency cash will give you some breathing room.

For instance, if you have $50,000 of living expenses every year, keep another $50,000 in the bank for emergency use.

Whenever you have more than this, you can think about putting the surplus into additional investments. A good rule of thumb is to wait until the sum in your bank accounts and currency market funds gets to be more than 15 months of living expenses, then chop it down to 12 months and put the rest into more investments.

So if your living expenses are $50,000 a year (or $4,166 a month), once you accumulate $62,490 you will have $12,490 to spend on stock.

But make sure to consider whether your cost of living might increase for the following year. Prepare a month-to-month income and spending plan detailing all your costs, variable and fixed, and anticipated income from dividends and other sources. This lets you check whether your income will cover your costs every month and determine the amount you can reinvest.

Keep proper records, using an Excel spreadsheet to record prices paid for stock, dividends received, capital gains, and whatever other data you will need for tax and planning purposes.

Dividends are taxed at a lower rate than interest, and when you're relying on them you don't have to worry about the share price. You'll hold the stock for as long as dividend payouts stay sensible, so it doesn't matter how much you could sell it for. Indeed, you'd like to see low costs on numerous stocks, since you're continually searching for a bargain. You can purchase more dividend-paying stocks in a low market and get more shares for your money.

Chapter 2 – Buy a Rental Property

Purchasing a rental property can be an awesome approach to generating passive income while you sleep. You profit by collecting rent money from the tenants and also when the market value of your property increases. As indicated by Property Observer, the normal yield on Australian rentals was 3.7% for houses and 4.5% for units.

When purchasing a rental property, one of the principle things to consider is whether the normal rental income will exceed your mortgage payments. If it does, your rental property will be income positive.

When an investment property is income positive, the rental profit is higher than the advance expenses. This is not always the situation; a few investors depend on the property increasing in value instead of on the rental income for their profit.

To determine whether a rental property is likely to be income positive, take a look at normal rents for comparable properties in the same area. You can get this information from a real estate agent or from real estate websites. If the rents you're seeing are higher than your advance costs would be, it's probable that the property you're considering will be income positive and you'll be able to relax while raking in the rental dollars.

Features of a Profitable Rental Property

There is a ton of work to be done between the decision to put your resources into real estate and actually purchasing your first rental property. Many first-time real estate investors are overwhelmed, because owning rental property is a complicated undertaking, full of landmines that can destroy your profits.

Start Searching

You might need a real estate agent to help you close the deal, but you ought to begin searching for your investment all alone. Having an agent can lead to unnecessary pressure to purchase before you have found a property that suits you. When you're looking, the most vital thing is having a good way to evaluate all of the properties and neighborhoods inside your investment range.

Aside from your budget, your investment range will be restricted by whether you plan to manage the property yourself (be a landlord) or hire someone to oversee it. If you plan to manage your own investment, you shouldn't get a property too far from where you live. If you are going to get a property management company to take care of it for you, that will be less of an issue.

Now let's investigate the main things to consider when searching for the right rental property.

Neighborhood: Where you purchase will determine what types of tenants you attract and how regularly you face vacancies. For instance, if you buy something close to a college, your potential tenants will mostly be college students, and vacancies will frequently occur right after graduation.

Rents: Rents are your bread and butter in this passive income method, so you have to understand what the normal rent in the area is. If charging the normal rent is not going to be sufficient to cover your mortgage payments, taxes and other costs, then you need to continue looking.

Thoroughly evaluate the area in order to gauge where it will be going in the next five years. If it looks like it's going downhill, then rents are going to decrease and what could be a reasonable purchase now may mean bankruptcy later.

Natural Disasters: Insurance is another cost for property owners, so it's crucial to know how much and what kind you would need to carry. If a region is prone to earthquakes or flooding, paying for the additional protection will make your investment less profitable.

Property Taxes: Property taxes vary, and you need to know what they would be on any property you're considering. High property taxes may not be an awful thing if rents are also high and the area attracts long-term tenants, but these don't always go together. The city assessor's office will have all the relevant data on this.

Schools: If the property you're looking at is suitable for families with children, it's best if it's also close to a nice school. If it is, you can charge higher rents, and its value is more likely to increase over time. If there isn't a school nearby, or if the local school has a poor reputation, the property may not be worth your while.

Amenities: If the neighborhood has a movie theater, public transport hub, mall, gym or park (or will soon get one), the property will pull in renters more easily. In larger cities, each neighborhood may have promotional literature that will give you an easy source of information on this type of thing.

Future Development and Building Permits: The municipal planning department will have data on new construction that has been proposed or approved for a given area. If there are numerous new condominiums, business parks and shopping centers going up in the general vicinity, it is most likely a decent investment proposition. However, keep an eye out for new development that could hurt your own investment. Lots of new apartments could mean more competition for renters, for instance.

Number of Vacancies and Listings: An abnormally high number of listings for a specific neighborhood can flag an area that has "turned sour" – or it could just indicate a seasonal cycle. Make sure beyond any doubt which it is before you purchase there, and remember that even if it is seasonal, you will have to figure out whether you can absorb those fluctuations and still make a profit.

The opening rates will give you an idea of how easy it will be to pull in tenants, and how much you can charge them. High vacancy rates force landlords to lower rents, while low opening rates have the opposite effect.

Crime: No one wants to live in an area where crime is a big problem. Go to the police for crime statistics; it's a lot more reliable than asking the seller. Things to search for are vandalism, curfew violations and petty crimes. While you're there, ask about police presence in the neighborhood.

Job Market: Locations with good employment opportunities tend to pull in more people – meaning more tenants. To discover how a specific zone rates, go to the Bureau of Labor Statistics or your neighborhood library.

If a large company is moving into the neighborhood, it will bring workers with it. This will almost always raise both rents and property values.

Getting Information

Talk with tenants and property holders in the area. Leaseholders will be significantly fairer about the negative aspects. If you are seriously considering a specific neighborhood, try to visit it at various times on various days of the week to see your prospective neighbors in real life.

The Physical Property

The best rental property for beginners is an apartment unit or a single-family dwelling. Apartments are not costly to maintain because the condominium association is there to maintain the building and all you have to worry about is the interior. On the other hand, since they're not detached housing, they have lower rents and appreciate more gradually than single-family homes.

Single-family homes tend to pull in longer-term leaseholders, usually families and couples. Because of their dual incomes, these people are more likely to be financially stable and pay the rent on time, so they make good tenants. As a landlord, you need to find a property and an area that will attract this sort of demographic.

When you have the area narrowed down, search for a property that has [appreciation](#) potential and decent anticipated income. Look at properties both within your budget and a little higher – real estate frequently sells for less than its asking price. Watch the prices of different properties and find out how much they last sold for to get an idea of current opinions about the area. You are searching for a property that, with a fresh coat of paint and a little remodeling, will pull in tenants willing to pay higher rents. You'll be able to recoup those initial expenses when you eventually sell the place.

As to cash flow, you must make an [informed guess](#). Take the normal rent for the area and subtract your monthly mortgage payments, property taxes (divide the annual figure by 12 months), and costs for maintenance and repairs. Make sure you budget enough for the last item; you'll be sorry if you don't. If you're left with a decent profit, you can now get a real estate agent to make an offer – and if everything goes well, print business cards with Landlord as your job title.

Chapter 3 – Earn Royalties

Can you write a love story? Or shred a guitar? You can make passive income from these skills through royalties. A royalty is a payment you get for somebody utilizing your creative work. Artists, musicians and authors all receive royalties. They enjoy a continuous stream of cash as people listen to their music, watch their films or purchase their books.

You can do it as well. There are various ways for you to start getting royalties. You could dress up and become YouTube star, share your recordings and get paid for impressions and promotions. If you don't look good on camera, you could sell other media online through sites like Shopify and FetchApp.

Even if you have no creative talent whatsoever, you can still profit from royalties by purchasing the rights to royalties from other individuals. The owner sells you the right to collect their future royalties for a fixed sum of cash. You can find royalties for sale on Royalty Exchange.

Ways to Make Money from your Songs

Many musicians struggle with getting airplay for their songs, submitting them to many different radio stations with no luck. What do you do next? If you're serious about making money from your songwriting, there are still numerous alternatives.

For now, you should know that there are two basic types of royalties that you can get from a song. One is the "mechanical" royalty and the other is the "publishing" royalty. Different countries have different terms for these, but the idea is the same everywhere.

The "publishing" royalty goes to the people who wrote the music and lyrics for a song. Those people are considered to be the ones listed when the tune is registered, so you have to be very careful during the registration process to make sure that each name listed is there by merit. This is especially so if you use a publisher to register your song. Some unscrupulous publishers exploit new artists by persuading them that it is standard practice to include the publisher's name on the registration! This implies that they co-own your music forever. Even if you fire that publisher later on, they still claim to co-own your music. A few publishers profit from forcing artists to "purchase" their own music from them.

The other royalty is the "mechanical" royalty, which refers to a recording of your music rather than the tune itself. Normally, whoever pays for the recording session gets part of this royalty, while the rest is divided among the musicians and vocalists featured on the recording.

If you record a cover of a Jim Rev melody and release it, you will get a "mechanical" royalty and Jim Rev will get the greater part of the "publishing" royalty because he composed the tune. Likewise, if anyone ever covers a tune that you wrote, they will get the mechanicals, and you will get the greater part of the publishing royalty.

Of course, the best thing is for you to compose your own melodies and play them so you get both of the royalties!

Before you can collect any royalties, you have to register your music with your country's music rights association or other appropriate body. As noted above, publisher can do this for you if you want.

Getting your music on the radio is the most straightforward and quickest way to royalty riches; you can make a whole lot of money if you have a hit single. Be that as it may, getting on the radio is not by any means the only way to profit as a musician:

Here are some effective approaches to profit from your music.

Public Performance

You are owed a royalty for each time your music is played in a public performance. Yes, that means that each time your band plays your own tune at a live music venue, you are earning a publishing royalty. Getting that royalty might seem like a lot of work, but it is actually very simple.

You should be industrious and fill in the Public Performance Publishing forms (accessible free from your country's music rights association website) after each gig with a rundown of the tunes that you played. Submit them legitimately, and voila! You get a little sum for every show, and the more gigs you play, and the more of your own music you play, the more you make!

Streaming Mechanicals

Streaming is becoming an increasingly prominent way of disseminating music. Legal streaming music is so widespread these days that your music is sure to find a place. Streaming services include Deezer, Rhapsody, Spotify, Simfy and more. They are not difficult to get on to (much simpler than a radio station) as their playlists are boundless, and you get a royalty each time your music is streamed (just like you would if it were played on the radio).

YouTube

There are so many ways to profit from your music on YouTube that I could devote a whole book to them. One of the simplest is to register with one of YouTube's distribution partners, for example, Rumblefish. You profit for every license, and the more you compose, the more you present, the more you can make. Examine this closely, as more than a few songwriters make a living from YouTube alone.

Selling your tunes to artists

Not every musician can compose great music. If you are a gifted songwriter, then get yourself a decent publisher who can help you pitch your songs to different artists. Attempt to hook up with established artists, since all it takes is one hit single from an established artist, singing the music that you composed, for you to begin seeing some weighty royalty checks in the mail. Aside from that immediate benefit, it enormously improves your recognition as a songwriter and your chances of working with different artists.

TV Syncs

This is the absolute best and speediest way to profit from your songwriting. Brands making commercials for television or radio are always eager to discover appropriate musical accompaniment. What's more, they're willing to pay for it.

If they want to use your music, they will license it for a certain period of time. When that time ends, they will have to pay you again for another license.

So think about writing songs that will appeal to top brands. If you can find a fit, you will begin earning some genuine cash from your music.

I trust this has helped a little bit, although it feels like I'm simply hitting the tip of the iceberg on the theme of how to make passive income from music. Still, we're not all musicians, so on to the next chapter…

Chapter 4 – Earn Interest

This one is crystal clear. If you have cash, put it in the bank, in a term deposit or savings account. Simple passive income!

Opening a bank account is genuinely simple, but figuring how to set aside the cash can be a challenge. From deciding where to cut spending to falling into the trap of immediate retail gratification, saving cash can be a mental struggle.

Think of a savings account as a credit to a bank. Banks take that cash and loan it to another person. They make a profit on the difference between what they pay you for the money (near 0%) and what they charge borrowers (typically more than 15% on credit cards). Decent business! But why give banks a 0% long-term loan? And yet this is exactly what happens with "sticky retail deposit," which is the banking term for account holders who put their cash in a savings account and never touch it.

Fortunately, numerous online banks now give up to 0.9% interest, and by utilizing my basic tenets, you can begin getting an even better return on your cash.

The best place to get interest is in a savings account. Don't waste your time searching for a checking account with a better than average interest rate.

Here are some tips for picking the best savings account to get the highest interest from your bank.

- Make sure beyond any doubt your money is FDIC insured. All US bank deposits are guaranteed up to $250,000; if you want to deposit more than that, open accounts at various banks.
- Try not to withdraw more than six times a month, because then fees start to kick in. For more consistent access, open a money market account, which is likewise FDIC insured.
- Ensure the interest compounds daily. Every day you get interest on a higher balance, which includes the interest earned the previous day.
- You needn't bother with a traditional branch bank for your savings account unless you write many cashier's checks or have an enormous deposit. The rate contrast between traditional banks and online banks is enormous!
- Before you open a Certificate of Deposit (CD), determine the amount of interest you relinquish for early termination. By law, this can be up to six months.

How to Trick Yourself into Saving Money

With wages down and prices up, it is difficult to save money. Following quite a while where household cash reserves were near zero, Americans are getting smart about their money again: even though the economy is still in a bad spot, the United States Department of Commerce says we're saving at a rate of 6.4%. Not terrible anymore, but there's still room for improvement. Here are five ways to start saving more.

Go On Autopilot

Ever heard the expression "pay yourself first?" It's the best way to get into the habit of saving: when you pay your bills come payday, top up your savings account like it's just another bill. Set up a different account for emergency funds. It's best to set up an automatic transfer to these accounts for payday, so you're not tempted to spend the cash somewhere else.

Keep the Change

Empty your wallet of loose change a couple of times a week and put the money in your savings account. Do it for a year and you'll have a couple of hundred dollars extra. It's another easy way to save money, and you'll come to love those pennies that used to clutter up your wallet.

Forget the Raise

Got a raise? Congrats! Before you begin spending it, expand your automatic transfer to your savings account to reflect that boost in pay. If it's a cost of living raise, you were already spending the extra money, and if it's a promotion related raise, you won't miss the cash you never had before.

Rather than spending your additional income, put it towards something that is critical to you, your retirement savings.

Keep the Habit

It took you years, but you at long last paid off your car. Rather than spending the additional money you now have every month, pretend you're still making those payments – just make them to your savings account instead of your lender. If you're truly looking ahead, you can set the cash aside until you need to replace your car. Imagine heading off to the dealership years from now and paying cash money for your next car – now there's some inspiration to keep those payments going into your savings account!

That rebate check, the $20 in your winter coat, that unexpected tax refund... Rather than blowing this cash on your favorite vice, put it into your savings account. You won't miss it, and it'll get you nearer to your objective, accumulating interest.

Saving cash doesn't need to be troublesome. With these tips, you can take the work out of putting cash aside, putting you on the path to achieve your financial objectives much faster than you would have thought.

Chapter 5 – Sell Yourself

You are your most important brand, and how you present yourself will eventually dictate your success or failure.

Your brand is your indispensable quality. The brand conveys who you are, what you're best at and how you can help other people in your journey through life. It's the way you will put your mark on the planet.

The advantages of a good personal brand are numerous; here are just a few:

- You won't have to apply for jobs – people will search you out for work
- You can pick your projects so you only do the things that interest you most
- Since there are always business opportunities for good brands, you won't need to worry about recessions
- You will stand out among your colleagues and peers
- You can charge a premium for what you are

Developing a good personal brand appears to be almost imperative. But how can you do it? Here are the essential steps I've found to kick your brand out of the park. They are not tasks to be checked off as much as they are lifestyle elements. Most cost only little money. The main investment is your creativity and time, and given the payout, I can't imagine a superior place to allocate those resources.

While companies have always tried to maintain a good public image to help them succeed, today, every entrepreneur also needs to manage their very own brand. Given that information is so widely and immediately shared on the web, it's scarily easy for even the most brand-wise person to wind up being depicted in ways that are either incorrect, or worse, damaging.

Fortunately, there's a demonstrably effective methodology you can use to fabricate an appropriate and dynamic reputation that is ideal for you and your company. This procedure, which comes from product services, starts with the acknowledgment that you are much more than a brand; in the way you are thought of and talked about by others, you are actually a product. This realization dictates the way you should showcase yourself, regardless of your objectives.

For instance, if you were advertising a brand on the web, you would concentrate on shaping important messages (e.g., Joe Jobs is known as an entrepreneur who is fixated on perfection). You would be concerned mainly with the language used to describe you and who you are and where that conversation takes place. But marketing yourself as a product means talking about the specific things you actually do — your features and functionality — along with how these add value to your potential clients and colleagues, your profession and your community (e.g., Joe Jobs leads the world's most inventive companies which regularly yield higher-than-forecast dividends).

Below are the proven steps you should follow to present yourself as a product.

Idea Generation: Conduct some research into famous brands and find individuals who are considered profoundly effective. With these findings close by, consider your own particular qualities and weaknesses, as well as your present opportunities and dangers. Lastly, come up with realistic dreams of you as a product —the things that you will do and how that fills a specific business sector's needs.

Assessment and Prioritization: Next, get some feedback on the ideas that you created in the primary stage. Utilize colleagues and partners to help you figure out whether what you plan to do is really in accordance with who you are. This is one of the most basic steps when characterizing yourself as a product. To make yourself into an effective product, you have to know your actual abilities and how you approach issues.

Product Development: When you figure out what you want to do, begin pulling together the assets required to manufacture yourself as an attractive product. That means gaining new abilities, acquiring accreditations, and finding the people or associations that will have a part in promoting you. For instance, contact partners and have them compose good testimonials for you on your LinkedIn profile. You should likewise be creating and testing the sorts of messages that you will need to highlight while advancing yourself.

Launch: Now that you're a versatile and tested product, it's time to introduce yourself to the business sector that will gain most by what you do. Assemble people's initial impressions to learn how you are being seen. Figure out whether you are being embraced by your market.

Refine: Refine your core offering in view of the outcomes from the launch point. Refinement and modification are vital to the lifespan of a product; the iPod has already gone through twelve iterations, for instance. Responding to criticism and keeping a promise to continually improve has made the iPod a game changer. It's the same when you characterize yourself as a product.

These steps will help you transform yourself into a product that everybody needs.

Transforming yourself into a personal brand is about getting your customers to recognize what you are about and realize what's in store when they get you. I am not almost where I need to be; rather, I work each day to arrive. So here is my rundown of five simple things you can do to help the process.

Be Real: No one likes a fake. You know what I mean – the individual who seems to be putting on an act. But (especially if you're collaborating on the web) it is hard to ensure that others really get what you are trying to say and there are no suspicions or misconceptions.

So if you need to differentiate yourself, make a point of being legitimate. Show people who you truly are, be straightforward, be open, and do what your mother taught you... tell the truth! Share what's happening in your own life. If you pull back the curtains, even only a tiny bit, to show people the personal side of you, they will feel like they are working with somebody they know.

Another part of being real is separating yourself by being unique. Discover your niche and become the best person within it. If you can do that, you are on the road to name recognition – or if I might venture to say it, brand recognition!

Take part in social media: Online networking is a big thing right now, and everybody is attempting to make sense of where they fit in on the web. If you need clients to discover you... if you need people to collaborate with you... if you need to be heard, you should be where everybody is – and that is on the web.

So open a Twitter account or two. Open a Facebook account. Open a YouTube channel and start posting videos. Start a blog and discuss your thoughts. Use your real name for everything, and post a decent picture of yourself. Discuss personal things in this forum, too. As I always say, people need to work with people, not business. Give others some knowledge of who you are, and they will be more inclined to work with you.

Share what you know: You've known about the importance of sharing since kindergarten. Offer more to others than what is given to you. You probably know some people you can count on for anything, ones who will always support you. Be that kind of person yourself. Just as nobody likes a fake, no one likes a taker.

If you catch wind of something truly cool that others could profit by, educate everybody about it. Make posts on your blog, make tweets, and share links on Facebook. Offer more to your group than you take. It might be an age-old adage, but it is still valid: people couldn't care less how much you know, until they discover how much you care. Offer what you know, and others will search you out.

Be the Expert: Odds are there's something you're great at. I don't know what that is, but you do. Capitalize on that to transform yourself into a brand. If you know more about a subject than anybody else, that's something valuable. Match this with the other things I am discussing here, and you'll have something that people need. Turn into a specialist at what you do. Give them something they can't get anyplace else. Remember to keep abreast of the latest developments in your niche, and read everything you can about it.

Think about the patterns, the new factors, and the people and companies that are at the front line of what you do. Google Alerts and Google Reader are great for keeping on top of what's happening in your area of expertise. I use them daily. Try not to work yourself to death. Use tools to help you save time, and invest a greater amount of your energy in collaborating with people.

Talk about Others: This might be the hardest part of my advice. Everybody's at least a little vain, and we naturally want to talk about ourselves... what we think, what we know, and how we feel. So it's not always easy to talk about others. But if you want to become a brand, you need to put others before yourself. You need to discuss other people more than you discuss yourself. If you do that, people will notice and appreciate it. They'll say things like, "That person is truly pleasant. He thinks more about other people than himself."

The following are some ways to sell yourself with minimal upfront time investment.

Sell Digital Files on Etsy: I've been into home style lately, and I swung by Etsy to find precisely what I needed. I ended up getting digital files of the work of art I needed printed out. The seller had made a cluster of wall art, digitized it, and was selling it on Etsy for download. There are other kinds of digital files on Etsy too, monthly planners, for example. If you're into graphic design, this could be an astoundingly easy income idea for you.

Sell an eBook Online: Self publishing is pretty common now. When you buy an eBook on Amazon there's a decent chance you're purchasing an independently published book. Self publishing is a very simple procedure. To publish a book yourself, you'll need to write and edit it, make a cover, and then transfer it to a system like Amazon's Kindle Direct Publishing. Don't expect your book to become a bestseller overnight, though. There's a lot of promotional work involved before you can transform this into an easy income stream.

Create a Course on Udemy: Udemy is an online platform that offers video courses on a wide array of subjects. Instead of being a student on Udemy, you can be a teacher. Make your own video course and sell it. This is an awesome opportunity if you are very knowledgeable in a particular topic, and it can be a great way to transform tutoring into a passive income stream!

Sell Stock Photos: Do you ever wonder where blogs, websites, and magazines get their photographs? These are typically purchased from stock photograph sites. If you do photography you can upload your photographs to a stock photograph website and get a commission each time somebody buys one of them.

Licensing Music: As discussed in Chapter 3, you can earn royalties and licensing fees from your music when it's played, performed, or used in YouTube videos or advertisements.

Create an App: Apps are extremely popular; think about how many you have on your cell phone or tablet. If you've ever had a good idea for one, why let it go to waste? You can hire a software engineer to make your app, then sell it on the App Store or Google Play for residual income.

Chapter 6 – Start A Blog

Anybody who tells you there's no cash in blogging is just plain wrong. According to a report by Online Income Teacher, the top-ranked Huffington Post site made a profit of $29,896 every day!

You might not be able to create another Huffington Post, but even the less well known blogs in the report made a lot of money – and the report only discussed a small portion of the blogs out there.

Starting to blog isn't that difficult; in fact, you can do it in about four minutes. It does require diligent work and effort to make your blog bear fruit, but once you're there you can fall asleep every night knowing that your blog will be making money while you're in bed.

What is blog?

A blog is an accumulation of content that is organized by date. This content can be words (copy) and also rich media (embeddable objects, video and audio). A blog normally concentrates on a specific topic. It can be built manually by composing the post, uploading it to a site by means of FTP, and distributing it. Alternatively, a blog can be managed by software called CMS (Content Management System), which automates many of these tasks.

Blogs can be read in several ways – by categories, tags, single post pages, home pages, syndication technologies, and also via RSS. Readers can subscribe to the blog and can sometimes help expand the content through various applications, devices, and tools. Blogs can also take the form of microblogging (like Posterous, Tumblr, and Twitter), video blogging, and other specific formats or content types.

Types of Blogger

There are seven types of blogger. Read on to find out which type you might be.

The Niche Expert

These bloggers build niche websites for anything that may have a decent profit potential –credit cards or gadgets or celebrities, for example. They run loads of advertisements, or put in a lot of member connections, or both. The quality of the content on these blogs varies, but the best niche specialists are profoundly motivated and driven and give genuine value to their readers.

The Business Owner

This is a fast-growing blog category. These bloggers aim to deliver amazing content to bolster their business (which could be anything from running a pub to SEO). Their posts may cover a variety of subjects, but all will somehow connect with their business.

These bloggers often have some of the best content on the web. They have a reputation to keep up, and they set themselves high standards. They see their site not as their business per se, but rather as a showcasing tool for their business.

The Professional Blogger

For the professional blogger, on the other hand, the blog is essential to their business. They're proud of what they've put together, and they love to expand on their favorite topics. Unlike niche experts, they rarely have multiple blogs.

They use their blogs to make money in different ways: eBooks, e-courses, consulting, membership sites, and/or other digital products. Unlike business owners, they don't tend have an offline presence like an office or store that you can visit. Their content is incredible – it must be, as it's the foundation of their business.

The Journal Writer

These bloggers keep old school blogs – ones like personal journals, covering a wide variety of topics, frequently in a narrative format.

They're often into memes, and may have little or no readership. Many post unpredictably, sometimes every day, sometimes not for months; others adhere to a consistent schedule.

They usually don't care about monetization or SEO. They may run a couple of advertisements or pop in some partner link to pay their hosting costs – but their blog is principally a hobby and a place to have fun. They consider readers to be potential new friends, not potential clients.

The Platform-Builder

These bloggers are hoping to become famous. Cash is a goal too, but a far-off one. They may be authors building a readership for their books, or people working in new media who want to impress their bosses.

Platform builders, like business owners, have a solid motivator to deliver extraordinary content. They will ordinarily stick reasonably close to one theme. You won't usually see advertisements on their blogs, and some will even stay away from affiliate links.

The Product Promoter

These bloggers have something to offer, frequently a book. You'll discover them anywhere but on their own website – and some won't have a website at all. Rather, they're on a blog tour around the web, contributing guest posts and comments in various places.

Product promoters may not even consider themselves to be bloggers, particularly if they don't have their own blog. They'll frequently have awesome experiences to share, but some might not know standard web composition techniques. Host websites can help by doing a touch of additional formatting on their guest posts.

The Freelancer

These bloggers get paid to write posts for someone else's website. They may spend all their time on a specific subject (personal development, gardening, healthy eating) or they may take whatever comes along. Many write consistently for the same website, frequently on a monthly or weekly basis.

Their content is generally top-notch – after all, they're being paid for it! Their employer will frequently do some editing to ensure the final piece reads well. These freelancers may have their own blogs, too; if they do, you'll likely see a "hire me" or "services" page there.

How to have a Popular Blog

Blogs are one of the most rapidly developing forms of mass communication. They first became popular in the 2000s following coverage in newspapers and magazines, and now a few famous blogs match such conventional media outlets in terms of readership, and, apparently, cultural relevance. The "blogosphere" has influenced corporate policy and elections, and some websites have a huge number of daily readers.

Below are some tips for creating a popular blog.

Decide what kind of blog to create: Choose a good niche and pick an appealing title that captures the quintessence of your blog. Keep in mind that a blog, like your clothes, is an extension of you. Your website may become the main thing the vast majority of people know about you, so you need to make certain that it reflects your inner mind.

Choose how regularly you will post: Some claim that posting frequently is ideal, saying that three quick posts a day are much more powerful than longer posts at regular intervals. The reality is that updating a blog with quality content every other day will get you a bigger number of readers than adding a few puff pieces daily.

That's important to keep in mind – the content matters! Whatever you do, remember that most readers prefer quality over quantity when perusing blog posts. When you begin, you'll find that you draw in a specific readership, which may be different from what you expected. In that case, you may need to modify how you work your journal to keep the readers you've gotten.

Get a few things together ahead of time: Creating a popular blog doesn't happen without any preparation. It's a good idea to assemble around a month of material before you let anybody know about your blog. Just begin writing; fame can wait for a while. Don't hesitate to go back and rework entries as needed even after you open up to the world. You can change anything whenever you want with most blog sites. The quintessence of a blog is making it your own. Work it how you feel is right.

Tell your friends about the blog: This helps grow your audience, but don't push too hard. They may feel you're just looking for compliments and attention and end up ignoring your blog. Remember, blogging is about you, and the more thought you put into it, the more people will take note.

Find popular blogs and comment on them: Read and post to them religiously. Make sure your comments are relevant, or they may be deleted. Don't expect miracles, but if you post interesting comments, they'll probably prompt at least a few people to visit your blog. (When you make comments on another blog, a link back to your own site will usually be included.) The more comments you make, the more people you can draw to your blog, but remember that nobody likes spam.

Read the terms of service carefully before choosing a blogging platform; once you begin using the site, you'll be held to its policies. [Click here for more blogging information](#) for beginners.

Ways to profit through blogging

You can profit online in many ways, but blogging can be exceptionally lucrative. After you've figured out how to begin blogging, it's also a great deal of fun to express your thoughts to the world. Many people derive a lot of satisfaction from it. But if it doesn't make money, you're still stuck with your day job! I know you're interested in passive income, so let's discuss some simple ways that you can profit from your blog and construct your financial independence!

Text Ads and Banners:

Banner ads can be super lucrative and truly help you profit from your blog, but they're not the easiest thing to get off the ground. The range from simple logos to larger promotions.

Let's assume ABC Health Foods wants to pay you x dollars a month to put their logo on your site. This is what a banner advertisement is.

That may sound simple, but there is a significant entry barrier, i.e., you have to assemble an audience before ABC will offer to pay you a dime. Many promotion systems require that you have no less than 100,000 page views every month. Furthermore, the vast majority of them pay very low rates in most niches.

A text advertisement is like a banner advertisement except you are just putting text on your site. This is not the same as a paid link, which I highly discourage!

The distinction can get blurry, however. Basically, if somebody wants to purchase a link placement, you ought to be careful. Yes, it's income sans work, but if web indexes like Google catch on to what's happening, your site could be cruelly punished with a lowered ranking. Numerous website administrators have seen their once healthy traffic shrink to a trickle as a consequence.

Pay Per Click (PPC):

Pay Per Click (PPC) is the money an advertiser pays to Internet publishers and search engines for a click on their ads which redirects a visitor to the sponsor's site.

Google's AdSense system is the biggest player here. It's easy to get up and running as a publisher. You create an account, use their tools to fabricate a promotion code, and stick it into your site. Google pays you a certain amount every time people click on the advertisement. This is an awesome way to make passive income.

This system brings together site administrators and advertisers, and that means you have to split the profits. Google pays out 68% of the money they receive. That's almost a one-third commission; however, two-thirds of something is a lot more than 100% of nothing.

The advertisements are "logical," which means they are with regard to your site's content. They come in both banners and text, and in different sizes.

Yahoo and Microsoft used to have their own publisher programs, but have left that market. Yahoo recommends Chitika as a substitute.

Pay per click [blog ads](#) are great while you're building a sufficient audience to pull in direct advertisers – and that ought to be your objective!

Paid Product Reviews

Many people go online to see what others are saying about a product they're thinking about buying. Companies know this and are now paying bloggers to review their products. There's nothing wrong with this; simply be upfront that you are being paid for the review. Since 2009, the FTC has also required that online publishers and bloggers have a general disclaimer on this subject in their terms of use.

Amazon Affiliate Program

Amazon's is the granddaddy of [affiliate programs](#). It works like this: when somebody goes to your site, they see a little widget that says "Joe recommends this book on passive income." If they click on it and purchase the book, you get some cash.

Obviously nowadays Amazon sells a lot more than books, so you can promote almost any retail product this way. It's an awesome way to generate cash when you begin because it's so simple and there are always things to buy in your particular niche. The drawback of the convenience is that the payout is fairly poor, as low as 4%.

Sell Stuff on your Blog Site

This is my top-choice approach to profiting from your blog! For instance, if you have a dating blog with many committed followers and a lot of great posts, why not gather your posts together and sell them as a digital book?

A lot of websites like [Texts from last night](#) or [Chuck Norris Facts](#) make money this way. You could also create premium content accessible only to paying members. Viola, now you have passive income!

The numbers can increase drastically if you continue to offer substantial value and keep your audience fulfilled. This can prompt offline opportunities, for example, workshops, coaching sessions, and endorsements.

You can even hire ghostwriters to create content. That way, you just sit back, let them do their work, pay them a fixed sum, and then enjoy a possibly lucrative revenue stream in the future.

If you would prefer not to mess with selling your own items – on the grounds that it takes too much time to handle customer service, sales pages, web hosting, and content creation – just sell other people's stuff through affiliate programs.

Try to get some of the leading people in your niche to offer their items on your site for a commission. Ideally they have a turnkey system setup that will result in a high likelihood of purchases. Don't be a guinea pig to help an inexperience individual fine tune their sales process.

Many eBook writers will give you as high as 65% to 100% commission on every sale. (They profit with memberships and repeat sales). Use this to advantage when assembling your passive income stream!

Chapter 7 – Drop Ship

We're always hearing about people making money by selling their old junk, but what if you don't have any old junk you want to get rid of?

The answer is drop shipping. Drop shipping lets you sell a wholesaler's items without taking ownership. You're basically a middleman between the customer and the wholesaler. The way to succeed at this is to ensure you get good wholesale prices from the supplier and can create enough sales to make it worthwhile. Once you've built up a fair amount of traffic to your site, you can begin automating the procedures and let the money flow in.

Make the journey simple by hosting your store on [shopify](). There are a lot of sellers there who are effective drop shippers.

Basic effective tips to start a drop shipping business

These tips will walk you through the essential steps required for you to begin and maintain a good drop shipping business.

Search for a hungry market

Having the best product on the planet is worthless if nobody needs it. Don't decide what to sell until you have done enough keyword research (as the vast majority of your sales will come through online channels). One way to see whether there is any demand for an item is by checking whether there is any competition. Enter the keyword for the product in an internet search engine like Google. Do you see advertisements to one side of the results page? That is a decent sign that there is a market for that item. Also look on comparison sites to check whether there is anybody selling the product. This is only the beginning of your research.

Look for a trustworthy drop shipper

Next you have to look for somebody to supply you with the items you want to offer. Many portals have drop shippers that will provide you with this service. Get in touch with them and look for the profit margins, their shipping terms, returns policy, payment options and so forth.

Get a domain name

Once you have found that hungry market and a supplier to drop ship for you, the next step is to get a domain name. To make it easier to find your site using web indexes, use a keyword associated with the items you will sell. For instance, if you are offering fitness equipment, you could pick the domain name fitnessetoolsbox.com (if it's available). Picking a domain name like joestore.com won't help much.

Find a web store provider

This will save you time and money over building a site from scratch. Some web store providers charge monthly or yearly fees, and this gives you the ability to upgrade your site whenever you want instead of having to search for a web designer to satisfy your guidelines. From my experience, I can guarantee you that a customized site is the most ideal approach when you start.

Upload your products

After choosing your web store provider, start the procedure of uploading the items you will offer. It's best not to upload every one of the products you will sell before you launch your site. Why would that be? Because you want to be up and running as soon as possible, and this will enable you to tweak things to suit your customers' desires as you get feedback from the marketplace. On the other hand, if you can hire somebody to carry out this task, then don't hesitate to proceed.

Start Marketing Campaign

After launching your site, you need to send it as much traffic as you can (staying inside your budget, of course). There are different ways to do this, including PPC, article marketing, online networking, advertising on comparison websites, and posting helpful comments in blogs with links pointing back to your site. When you discover a technique that is bringing in great traffic and generating more sales, ease up on the others and focus on that one.

Do Email Marketing

There is a famous saying in the web advertising world that goes "the money is in the list." This is just as true for your drop shipping business site. Have a form on your site where guests can leave their names, email addresses and messages. You can then send bi-weekly or weekly messages with helpful tips, special offers, new product announcements, and so forth to your subscribers. You'll see a surge in sales every time you send these messages.

Chapter 8 – Earn Commissions Through Affiliate Marketing

This is like drop shipping in that you will be selling another party's items. You get automated income through your site by helping different people and companies to sell their products. How it works is that you earn a commission from the items that are sold as a result of clients coming from your site.

The best way to select affiliates is to search for companies who make products suitable for your existing audience or clients. Connect with them and ask how you can be an affiliate.

Basic effective method to make money as an affiliate marketer

Affiliate marketing is one way to get passive income online. An affiliate marketer promotes particular items or sites in return for a cut of the profits or commissions from the web traffic that comes from them. Whenever web traffic from an affiliate prompts a sale, the affiliate gets cash. At the end of the day, the products or services are provided by others; you're merely a sales or advertising outlet.

While there are no realistic get-rich-quick plans, many people earn easy income by doing web advertising as an affiliate. Understanding how to be an effective affiliate marketer can help you decide if a career in this possibly lucrative field may be a good fit for you.

Choose business models: There are two basic plans that beginning affiliate marketers choose between. You can have a review site or a resource site. Which one you choose will depend on upon your familiarity with the products or services you advertise.

Resource websites ordinarily put a vendor's site in affiliate links or banner ads inside articles and posts. This business model requires continuous overhauls and fresh content to ensure that clients come back to the advertiser's site on a regular basis.

A review website features reviews of products or services that the advertiser has tried and recommends. Every review incorporates a banner or link promotion that will take readers to the merchant partner's site. The upside of review sites is that they require fewer updates; you just need to make minor changes to ensure that search engines keep on listing your site in their results.

Have a website: To act as an affiliate marketer, you'll need your own platform (a website or blog) on which to post links and advertise services/products. If you already have a website or blog, you can utilize it to start gaining extra passive income as an affiliate marketer. If you don't yet, you should think about how to create one now.

The benefits of a blog site, for example, Blogger, are that it's easy to operate, and often free. Nonetheless, inexpensive websites like Hostgator and GoDaddy.com offer blog benefits and may look more professional than a personal blog.

Consider signing up with an affiliate marketing company. Although you'll eventually want to work autonomously, joining a company that has some expertise in web promotions is an easy way to enter the field of affiliate advertising. Companies like MoreNiche let anybody who wants to be an affiliate marketer to sign up for free. It's a convenient platform for publicizing services and products.

Some sites permit you to take part in pay-per-click affiliate marketing without running your own blog or website. Direct links through outside merchants' sites permit you to make and profit from advertisements without posting them to your own site. For example, you may create a promotion for a clothing site and publicize on it Facebook; when somebody clicks on your advertisement, they go straight to the clothing site, rather than the website you have created. Some companies with expertise in direct links include Affiliates Directory, Link Share, Associate Programs, and E-commerce Guide.

Select a Niche: Most affiliate marketers choose a niche, or area of specialization. Before you start advertising services or products, you'll have to find a good area to work in.

Your niche doesn't have to be anything you're already an expert in. You can pick a niche you're eager to learn more about, for instance. But getting started is a lot of work, so try to choose an area you'll be happy working in for the long term. Your best passive income profits come after you've gotten everything off the ground.

Choose services and products: Once you've selected a niche, begin looking for services and products to feature on your platform. What these will be, and also the amount of work you'll need to put in, will depend on your preferred niche.

Companies like Commission Junction are perfect for advertising traditional services/products. Commission Junction has a large scope of potential publicizing opportunities, so it's also good for newcomers to the field who haven't settled on a niche yet.

Marketers keen on digital content, like software and eBooks, may appreciate working with a company like PayDotCom, Clickbank, Amazon, or E-addict.

Pay-per-click (PPC) models like Google AdSense may please a few advertisers. PPC models pay significantly less than other marketing models, but they require less work from the advertiser. The advertiser's compensation is controlled by the amount of web traffic directed to the objective site.

Work with affiliates: Affiliates will develop your business and help you take advantage of web traffic. There are numerous approaches to meeting and drawing in affiliates, but the best way is simply by building a reputation for yourself. You can do this by creating a well-known blog, by gaining large numbers of online followers, or by publishing a popular article or book.

There are different methods for meeting affiliates, varying in their likelihood of success and how much energy they require. The essential strategy for getting affiliates ordinarily includes one of the following techniques:

- Emailing or otherwise reaching out to bloggers and online advertisers who share a common specialty and asking them to advertise your item or take part in mutually beneficial cross-promotion wherein both you and the other blogger promote each other's products.
- Finding good partners on the web, either through gatherings, shared contacts, or affiliate systems (for example, Commission Junction or Clickbank) that you can join online.

Direct people to your affiliate program: Once you've constructed a good platform and secured associates to work with, you'll have to direct people to your affiliate program. There are various approaches to this, but one of the least demanding and best techniques involves composing an article or blog post and using your email newsletter to welcome your supporters to join the affiliate system. Other strategies include:

- Giving unlimited free content to other websites – linked back to your site, of course.
- Using viral advertising, similar to the link toward the end of your newsletter that enables readers to pass the bulletin on rapidly and easily.
- Securing free links on high-traffic sites.

What to Expect

Expect a great deal of work. Many newbies go into affiliate marketing hoping to get rich quickly. But it takes a great deal of work to get things off the ground, particularly in the early stages. Some advertisers work eight hours a day, seven days a week as they attempt to build up and launch their platforms. Remember that the field is extremely competitive and many companies are managed by advertising professionals.

Know how it works: Affiliate marketers include their own affiliate's link in their own blog or webpage. The links don't have any effect on clients or on the cost of any services or products being offered by affiliates. Nonetheless, when the client makes a purchase by clicking a partner link inside a predetermined time frame, the advertiser gets a commission from that deal. The amount you earn will depend on each affiliate's costs, bonus rates, and the number of sales you can make on a monthly or weekly basis.

Understand your demographics: Each affiliate will have their own particular target demographic. As the partner advertiser, you must understand your demographics and tailor your reviews or advertisements in a manner that the targeted demographic will be reached through your platform. Knowing, for instance, the age, average income range, and interests of the target demographic will help you tailor your advertisements and reviews to that demographic.

Tips for Affiliate Marketing

Affiliate marketing is one of the speediest approaches to passive income; however, getting started with affiliate marketing is truly tough. You need to work extremely hard to make your first buck, but once you make it, things begin getting less demanding for you. And you don't need a degree in anything – all you need is an online forum or blog from which you can collaborate with individuals all over the globe. If you're still stressing, I have a rundown of tips for affiliate marketing:

Be Interactive: This is the most vital part of affiliate marketing because this is the main pathway toward making money. You have to be interactive if you hope to rake in heap of cash from affiliate marketing. Collaborate with your group via social networking sites, and answer all their comments and questions on your site.

Stay Reliable: This is also very important in affiliate marketing. Never flog shoddy services or products, even if they give you an immense commission! When you double cross your audience, they will never believe you again, and that will be the end of your affiliate marketing journey. So stay reliable and sell quality stuff, regardless of how much commission you get.

Continue Experimenting: You don't always hit the jackpot when you try something new (although you may!), but at the very least it will help you figure out how diverse projects work. Continue trying new affiliate marketing programs, because each one has its own unique strategies, and some of them will pay off in a big way. If you have a real interest in affiliate marketing, exploring different avenues is also just a lot of fun.

Be Patient: Persistence is a definite requirement in affiliate marketing. If you aren't persistent, you'll probably leave the affiliate marketing arena before you've recouped your initial investment and lose a lot of money. As I have said, almost all of your investment here takes place before you make your first buck. However, things continue getting simpler after that, so stay patient and stick to it.

Quality written content is the final deciding factor

Content is the engine behind affiliate marketing. I know some people whose objective with affiliate marketing is all about making fast money, but I always tell them not to sacrifice content quality to save a couple of dollars. This always decreases your traffic, and once it's gone – it's gone for good.

Chapter 9 – Sell Products On Niche Sites

It may take a while to find a niche where you can use your expertise to sell items for a healthy profit. Whether it's exercise equipment or custom jewelry boxes, the way to be profitable is to choose a niche you will be aggressive in. When you become master of that niche, there's nothing standing between you and a good stream of passive income.

Does making a lot of easy money from websites you can build and forget sound great? Well, that's what niche content sites are all about, so let's take a closer look.

The basic idea is straightforward. Do some research, look for some uncommon niches that aren't overcrowded right now, build a content site focusing on the niche using Chitika or a similar system, and simply let it stay there generating a few dollars every day.

Wait, a few dollars? Well, it's true that these sites don't usually make more than that – but there's nothing that says you can only have one. When you think about it that way, even $4 a day can be counted as a success. When you're making that much, you can proceed to establish your next niche content site.

If you create one site every week, by the end of the year you'll have fifty-two niche content websites. If they all make an average of $4 every day, that's $208 daily, and around $76,000 per year. And most of these sites won't require any updates at all; you finished your work when you found an undiscovered niche and filled it with content.

Getting Started

Before you focus on that end goal, you have to figure out how to effectively direct traffic (from search engines) to your chosen niche. You make your money when site visitors click your promotional links, and it turns out that first-time visitors click more ads than loyal readers. They'll find your site by accident, breeze through the content, click an advertisement or two, and most likely they'll never come to your site again.

People will only return to your site if there's new content, and if they're coming for the content, they're less likely to click your advertisements. It's not to your greatest advantage to have a loyal audience for your niche website. You don't need the obligation of posting fresh content in a niche you're not really interested in. Just think about how to draw new traffic, and forget the rest.

Finding a Niche

To begin with, then, you must find niches that do draw traffic. Use the standard tools, for example, Overture Keyword Data Miner, in order to conduct research on the number of searches made for certain keywords. Look for those with no less than 1,000 searches per month. Don't go for keywords and subjects that are too narrow; search for a niche that has some traffic but low competition.

Take the niche of Sump Pump Information. Do you know what a sump pump is? I don't, and I don't care. What's important is that some people search for information concerning sump pumps online. You just need a few of those people to click your advertisements every day.

The essential thing is to look for subjects that work with Pay-Per-Click and the various internet marketing strategies. A niche content website should allow connecting these two, and your own cash, with the assistance of web search tools for publicizing the site and traffic programs to monetize it.

Before starting any niche content site, be sure there are monetization possibilities; otherwise, you're wasting your time. Use Google to search for AdWord campaigns in the niche you are thinking about – if you see a few promotions targeting that niche on the right side, you know publicists are paying to target these business sectors.

To be truly careful, sign into AdWords and carry out some test campaigns to see what the offer costs are for the keyword research topics/subjects. If the costs are sensible, then there presumably is some competition for the keywords from publicists running AdWord campaigns.

Look for Competition

When you've identified a couple of niches you think possess some potential, search those keywords and see what results appear. If what shows up is poorly streamlined (low heading tag/poor title key phrases, low PageRank), you can be certain that a website with better content would rapidly bounce to the highest point of the search results. By "rapidly" I mean in around half a year (note that Google Sandbox will affect how quickly you attain high rankings). Now you have your first possibility for a niche content site!

Have a Website

I recommend using WordPress for your niche website. WordPress is blog management program that uses a MySQL/PHP backend. It's a very simple way to handle most of what you'll need to do with your site; usually you simply plug in the content and go. Sometimes, though, a static HTML website might be more appropriate, for instance when you just need a micro-site for a couple of webpages and it's quicker to set it up in HTML format. Just decide what works best for you and go with that.

Ways to find Content

You might assume this would be the most difficult part of the niche content website system – how can you come up with content for a niche which you have no enthusiasm for or involvement with? Well, it's not all that hard to blast out a couple of pages of relevant content using what's available on the web, but if writing really isn't your thing, try these options:

- Use articles from an open article repository, for example, Ezine Articles. Writers contribute articles to these websites, and you can copy them to your site as long as you keep the byline in place. The drawback is that anybody else can do the same thing, so the content won't be unique. But if your niche is small enough there won't be many other people interested in the subject, so if you're lucky enough to discover some on-topic content on a repository website, you can use it without worrying too much about this issue.
- Use freelancers: Freelancers around the world are anxious to take your cash in return for their written work. Upwork and fiverr are the biggest freelance hubs online, and posting an article writing project there will get you many responses. Most freelancers are really adroit at delivering content on any point, although you shouldn't expect it to be particularly original. A couple of thousand words shouldn't cost you a lot of cash. If you go this route, try to set up a long-term association with a decent freelancer who can help you with your future websites as well.
- Republish Wikipedia content: Wikipedia has grown so big that it now has entries for even very obscure niches, and the GNU Free Documentation License means you are allowed to republish them.
- Article subscription services: There are a few article services that give members the right to use their articles; some even guarantee a specific number of fresh articles in various niches over a certain time period. The idea here is that you get an article stream that few people have access to. The article service keeps it this way by limiting its membership to a few hundred. Of course, in the worst-case scenario, that could mean a couple of hundred niche websites using the same content! I've never used these sites, but I've read different reports about them, some great, some awful. Personally, I'm suspicious about the idea; I don't have a clue where they get the articles they supply to their clients, but I doubt very much it's from reputable authors.

Benefits Keyword Click Through Prices

For many niche content websites, AdSense or Chitika may be the primary monetization system. Click-through costs are determined based on advertiser interest. The best thing is to discover a niche with few established content websites but a considerable number of advertisers contending to attract clients. This implies click-through costs will be high, although the business sector is not likely to stay undiscovered for long and a group of competing content websites will probably appear soon. Truth be told, you may never discover this perfect combination.

A more probable situation is a niche with high click-through costs due to bunches of advertisers and a couple of entrenched content websites; or low keyword costs and no opposition. To profit in these circumstances you just have to be better at SEO than the other websites. You get more clicks if your website gets more traffic.

Avoid a niche that has a couple of advertisers with very low click-through costs. Regardless of the amount of traffic you manage to get and how much you master your niche, if no advertisers are paying to utilize Google AdWords, you won't certainly receive any income from AdSense, or it may be around 10 cents a day from the one advertiser that has no competition.

Note that Chitika can demonstrate cameras, computer systems and other electronic items that may appeal to many people and deliver enough click-through to make it advantageous. However, this may end up being a waste of time; if the niche is not important to the monetization technique, the profit you get will be exceptionally inconsistent.

The Achievers

There are two web advertising techniques I want to examine here, one called overachiever and the other underachiever.

Underachiever

Niche content site building is the prime example of the underachiever technique. Good niches will never be uncompetitive for long, and as niche content site building becomes better known you will certainly encounter rivals for your niches. Underachieving is when you decide to gently skim a niche, maybe by offering a digital book to a market that at present is not satisfied.

Niche content websites benefit the niche by providing essential data and create advertising revenue; there is no expectation of making a great profit from any one. The main aim is to repeat and develop an array of good niches. Thus you have to continue trying to find new fresh niches in order to supplant those that turn out to be excessively competitive, making it impossible to be profitable.

If you can juggle numerous websites and enjoy the challenge of learning a little bit about a wide variety of subjects, the niche content website procedure can work very well for you. If you can manufacture a truly substantial portfolio, it won't matter if one of your niches becomes unprofitable due to competition; it would take an awful lot to destroy your whole income stream.

The best approach is to regard niche content sites as training and research tools. Realize what you have to do to generate traffic to a website from a search engine. Figure out how to upgrade a website, find a good niche and construct content rapidly. When you discover a niche that has high demands and returns, you can consider changing your technique from underachiever to overachiever.

Begin gathering email addresses for a mailing list. Write eBooks, find partner items to sell, start a membership service, record videos to create information products, and venture to the marketplace. You've turned into the master of that niche, and now you can rely on it for long-term passive income regardless of competitor activities.

Overachiever

Overachieving is the point at which you dominate a niche, turn into a specialist and "dive deep" by offering more than one service or product. You can offer workshops, audio and video recordings, and an entire host of extra tools that can create faithful clients who are worth significantly more than a one-time purchase or content link advertisement click.

In a sense, this is a "loss leader" methodology. Creating good content, amassing physical inventory, and paying partner commissions is expensive, and you won't be in the black right away. But when clients get to be fans and buy everything you make, that will add up to a large amount of money over time.

Influence Previous Hard Work

Many of the wonderful and weird niches out there are currently dominated by extremely amateurish niche websites, maybe hosted on free servers with designs made in Microsoft Word. Although most of them have low PageRank, they may appear on top of the search results simply because of the absence of competition. A quick and simple procedure can push your well executed, high PageRanked website past these amateur efforts.

Most online advertisers focus on one website, likely their primary business or blog. This site appreciates great, hard-earned traffic and has bunches of backlinks that have been developed over time. Utilizing this website as an instrument to advance other websites is an excellent proposition, particularly in the niche content market.

Learning to cook vegetarian, how to snowboard, how to do magic tricks, where to find the best secondhand clothes, how to raise turtles – these are all things somebody cares about and will search for online. You must find the obscure, think outside of the box, and discover markets that you would never be part of yourself.

The good news is that the search engines are brimming with key phrases. You can simply fire up your web browser and start doing research. Follow the external links. Browse Wikipedia and extend your point of view. You may find many niches that could be exceptionally profitable that nobody else has considered.

Chapter 10 – Selling Information Products

Information products make not just streams but floods of passive income, that is, cash that flows to you whether you're working at your office, snoozing on the couch, or lazing on the beach. How? You make the product once and sell it again and again. You make an initial investment of money and time and afterward profit from the product. You can't do that with time; you can't sell an hour twice.

Simply put, an information product is anything that has been recorded in some fashion – whether that is video, print, or audio – so that it can be conveyed to others. There are many ways to sell and package information. The most common are:

- eBooks and print books
- Special reports and booklets
- Workbooks and manuals
- Subscription-based websites
- Downloadable audio files, CDs, or audio cassettes.
- DVDs and videotapes
- Teleclasses

The key is that you're taking the knowledge in your mind and transforming it into something that others can appreciate and utilize even when you're not around.

I've sometimes heard information products referred to as "artifacts." This term, which comes from archaeology, depicts an information product as something left for future generations.

The procedure you use to serve your customers, each story you gather from media sources, each past experience you carry with you, each unique thought you have, is a bit of information that can be recorded and shared.

How to Create Information Products

There are a couple of basic methods for creating information products to offer online.

Adobe PDF eBooks

The most effortless to make, from a technical perspective, is a digital book in Adobe Acrobat PDF format. Most word processors, including MS Word, can save your writings in PDF format. This can be anything from a 1-page checklist to a 20-page special report to a 100-page booklet to a 500-page novel.

Audio Recordings

Every PC sold nowadays can record sound. That means that once you've written your digital book, you can read it into your PC and your have another form of your information product!

You can also create sound recordings from tele-workshops you present. You may give a free tele-workshop as a lead-generation tool, or you may charge attendees a fee. Either way, you should record the workshop. Afterward, you'll be able to sell the recording to people who couldn't make it to the live event.

If you can convince a recognized expert in your industry to do an interview with you, an audio recording of your discussion will also have excellent sales potential.

Video Recordings

Using a webcam, you can record a video of yourself discussing a subject in which you're knowledgeable. If you can, it helps to include slides from a PowerPoint presentation; however, to do this you will need to have video-editing software, for example, iMovie for the Mac or Adobe Premiere Pro for Windows. To take your video to the next level, you can hire a videographer to record a live talk or workshop that you give. You may be able to cover his professional fee by selling tickets to the event. If not, try to find a student from a nearby visual arts school who will work for a reduced rate. You truly needn't bother with telecast quality video for this anyway, since it will in all probability be viewed on a PC screen.

You can also make videos using screen capture programs like Camtasia Studio (available for both Mac and PC).

The most effortless way I have found of making an information product is having a tele-seminar. You welcome maybe a couple of specialists on a subject and you talk with them. Most phone companies will permit you to record the entire thing, and afterward you can download it to your PC as an mp3 file. Now you have your first information product.

To take it to another level, you can enlist a transcriptionist to type the spoken words into a text file, which you can upgrade by editing and adding your affiliate links to the products or services mentioned in the interview. Now you have your second information product.

Selling Your Information Products Online

To sell your information products, you have to install a shopping cart module/plugin on your blog. Using your own shopping cart gives you the most flexibility, but it requires some specialized knowledge.

For payment handling I suggest PayPal. It's been around quite a while, is part of the eBay group, and works everywhere in the world. Another good thing about PayPal is that it doesn't cost you anything unless you make sales: there are no weekly/monthly charges or setup costs. All they take is a little commission for every sale, depending on your monthly volume.

When you've made your product and listed it on your site, it's time to promote it. Compose a blog post about it on your website; search for guest blogging opportunities; post to online social sites like Facebook and LinkedIn.

One of the best ways to make more sales is to enroll other people to sell your product for you: i.e., your affiliate network. To make an affiliate system on your WordPress-based online blog website I want to prescribe this simple [WordPress affiliate plugin](#). There are others, but this one is the best I've found, and functions admirably.

How to write effective sales copy

Make it scannable: Just as when you're composing a blog post, use headers, bullets and bolding, and separate the content with pictures.

Focus on advantages: Here's example of an advantage: "This video will answer all your inquiries and give you all that you need to take care of business, and you can watch it on any device."

Make it just the length it should be: Long sales copy is incredible for offering something expensive to somebody who doesn't have any acquaintance with you. However, if you're sending an email to people who are familiar with you and the topic, they aren't going to want to read 5,000 words to decide whether they want to spend $15 or $40 to tackle their issue.

Below are some tools that can help you sell your information product:

[Sendowl](#)

Plans begin at $9 per month.

Sendowl's two good qualities are its pleasant, simple-to-learn client interface and its links with various payment processors, including Stripe, PayPal, and Authorize.net. If you don't mind paying a membership charge and you want to offer clients the option of paying with PayPal or Visa, Sendowl is a decent choice.

[Gumroad](#)

With Gumroad, instead of paying a monthly membership, you pay a 5% commission in addition to $0.25 per sale.

Gumroad gives you the choice of sending people to a page or installing a link to your product page. You can receive money by means of credit cards. You get paid by means of direct deposit or PayPal at regular intervals. It's a decent choice for people who aren't sure what their monthly sales will be and would prefer not to focus on membership expenses.

[E-junkie](#)
Plans begin at $5 a month.

E-junkie was one of the first platforms to offer digital items, and it's still not an awful choice. The client interface could be more visually attractive, but it works, does well with PayPal, and has a reasonable entry-level plan to start you off.

Are you ready to start now?

Here's a fast look at what you have to do:

- Think about how to sound sensible when answering inquiries (audio, video or in writing) and package your answers.
- Choose how to offer your item.
- Monitor the inquiries you get from customers and potential customers, and consider alternate ways you could motivate them to buy a product (pre-work you do with clients or entry-level services you provide).
- See how it works!

You can refine your sales copy for the product after it's been on offer for a while, taking into account any criticism you get, but for the most part you simply need to get the item out there.

Try not to get hung up on perfection; there's always time for enhancing your product later. Information products are living documents, and you might as well start to profit from them by distributing a beta version at the earliest opportunity.

Conclusion

Your ability to generate passive income relies to a great extent on your audience. If they conclude you're more focused on making money than on serving them, you won't succeed. I've seen plenty of people try something only for the cash; they always fizzle out because their expectations aren't driving them along the right path. Make what you do about helping people and making them feel better. If you can do that, you'll be well on your way to generating passive income.

So there you have it, 10 good ways you can make passive income while you sleep. The important thing to remember is that you'll only get to that point if you're willing to invest some time, money and energy beforehand. Put in those brainstorming ideas and that hard work and gain those dollars.

Thanks for reading!

www.ingramcontent.com/pod-product-compliance
Lightning Source LLC
Chambersburg PA
CBHW050832180526
45159CB00004B/1871